ANALYZING ENVIRONMENTAL CHANGE

ANALYZING DISAPPEARING HABITATS

ASKING QUESTIONS, EVALUATING EVIDENCE, AND DESIGNING SOLUTIONS

PHILIP STEELE

Cavendish Square

New York

Published in 2019 by Cavendish Square Publishing, LLC, 243 5th Avenue, Suite 136, New York, NY 10016

Copyright © 2017 Wayland, a division of Hachette Children's Group

First Edition

Cataloging-in-Publication Data

Names: Steele, Philip.
Title: Analyzing disappearing habitats: asking questions, evaluating evidence, and designing solutions / Philip Steele.
Description: New York : Cavendish Square, 2018. | Series: Analyzing environmental change | Includes glossary and index.
Identifiers: ISBN 9781502639448 (library bound) | ISBN 9781502639455 (pbk.) | ISBN 9781502639462 (ebook)
Subjects: LCSH: Habitat conservation--Juvenile literature. | Wildlife conservation--Juvenile literature. | Endangered ecosystems--Juvenile literature. | Global warming--Juvenile literature.
Classification: LCC QH75.S834 2018 | DDC 578.68--dc23

Produced for Cavendish Square by Tall Tree Ltd
Editors: Jon Richards
Designers: Ed Simkins

Printed in the United States of America

CONTENTS

IT'S TIME TO TALK ABOUT
NATURAL HABITATS

When the health of the global environment is under threat, natural habitats are put at risk too. For example, the magnificent orangutan lives in the tropical rainforests of Borneo and Sumatra. About a hundred years ago, there were probably about 230,000 orangutans living in the wild. Today, there are only about 60,000 left, but even these are broken up into small groups, and their future is in danger. Their rainforest habitat has been destroyed by loggers and miners and replaced by commercial plantations of oil palms.

An orangutan in the tropical rainforest of Danum Valley, Borneo. This region is now a conservation area with a rich variety of plants and rare animal species.

THE CONNECTION

How has it come to this? You could blame governments. You could blame the loggers. You could blame the companies who use the oil made from the palm's pulped fruit. Or we could blame ourselves, because we buy palm oil every week at the supermarket. The oil is found in the biscuits, cakes, pies, chocolate bars, sweets, ice cream, soap, toothpaste, shampoo, and lipstick in our shopping carts. This is just one story of many. In fact, similar examples may be found all over the planet. Humans are destroying natural habitats and resources, often the same ones on which they themselves depend.

HUMANS RULE THE WORLD

The geological epoch or age in which we have been living since the last Ice Age is known as the Holocene (meaning "most recent"). But scientists are now calling for a new geological term to be used for the period starting in 1950 — the Anthropocene or "human" epoch. The global environment is now defined by humans and their activities.

TAR SANDS

The Athabasca oil sands in Alberta, Canada, provide bitumen, or very heavy crude oil. Extraction by surface mining, using vast amounts of hot water, damages the natural environment and emits high levels of greenhouse gases.

OPENCAST MINING

The Bingham Kennecott Copper Mine, near Salt Lake City in the US, is a massive human-made excavation. Mines like this have considerable impact on the surrounding environment.

OIL LEAK

An oil pipe in Russia leaks into the surrounding water and land. Oil leakages have serious consequences for plants and animals, and can take months or even years to clean up.

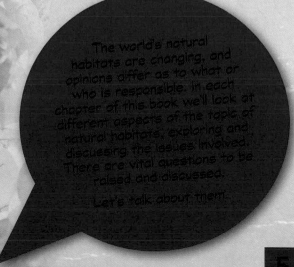

The world's natural habitats are changing, and opinions differ as to what or who is responsible. In each chapter of this book we'll look at different aspects of the topic of natural habitats, exploring and discussing the issues involved. There are vital questions to be raised and discussed.

Let's talk about them.

> "We cannot say we love the land and then take steps to destroy it for use by future generations."
>
> Pope John Paul II (1920-2005)

NATURAL NETWORKS

Life on Earth is powered by the Sun. Plants and animals form networks, which depend on each other. There are food chains and food webs linking animals that prey on each other. There are fungi that live on trees, fleas that live on hedgehogs and plants that feed on flies. There are flowers that need to be pollinated by bees so they can reproduce.

Arctic Ocean

Atlantic Ocean

Pacific Ocean

Indian Ocean

The Earth has eleven major land biomes, dominated by certain vegetation, from frozen polar regions to tropical rainforests, deserts, and mountainous areas.

Southern Ocean

THE HOME PLANET

These networks and the environment in which they operate make up an ecosystem. The environment is shaped and sustained by climate and by the water cycle, the ongoing pattern of rainfall, evaporation, and condensation. These create regional biomes, or life zones, such as tropical rainforest, hot desert, or grassland. The area where a particular animal or plant species makes its home is called a habitat. A rich variety of plant and animal species is called biodiversity.

60-80% pollinated by animals

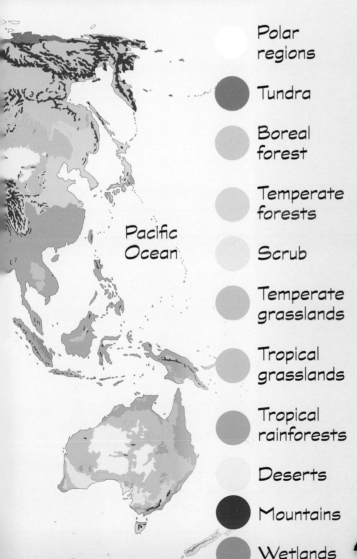

- Polar regions
- Tundra
- Boreal forest
- Temperate forests
- Scrub
- Temperate grasslands
- Tropical grasslands
- Tropical rainforests
- Deserts
- Mountains
- Wetlands

Pacific Ocean

NUMBER CRUNCH

60 to 80 percent of the world's flowering plants, including many crops, rely on pollination by animals for their survival.

BREAKING THE SYSTEM

If a habitat is altered, damaged, or destroyed, a plant or animal may drop out of one of the networks, such as the food chain. This has a domino effect on other species, and biodiversity is reduced. Many bees and other insects are currently in decline because of habitats being sprayed with pesticides. The insects pollinate many of the plants on which we and other animal species depend for our survival. We can thank bees for about one-third of our nutrition.

> "When we try to pick out anything by itself, we find it hitched to everything else in the Universe."
>
> John Muir, US conservationist, in *My First Summer in the Sierra* (1911)

AGAINST NATURE

Did you know that about 57,900 square miles (150,000 km²) of forest habitat is being lost to the world each year? All those trees could have been pumping out the precious oxygen that we need to breathe. The world's largest rainforest covers the Amazon river basin. It is home to a huge variety of species and has shrunk by about 17 percent in the last 50 years.

The Carpathian Mountains of Romania are being stripped of their trees. The forests are home to a variety of animal species such as the brown bear.

LOSS OF THE WILD PLACES

Half of the world's wetlands have been lost over the last 100 years and 27 percent of the oceans' coral reefs have gone. Habitat destruction is the main threat to 85 percent of the world's endangered species, according to the IUCN (the International Union for Conservation of Nature).

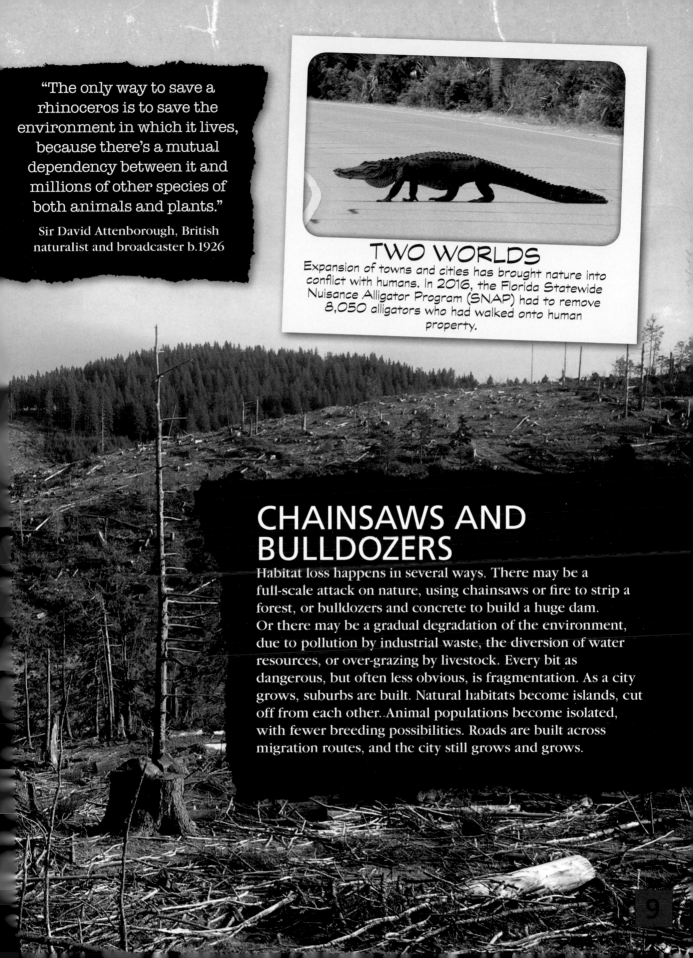

> "The only way to save a rhinoceros is to save the environment in which it lives, because there's a mutual dependency between it and millions of other species of both animals and plants."
>
> Sir David Attenborough, British naturalist and broadcaster b.1926

TWO WORLDS

Expansion of towns and cities has brought nature into conflict with humans. In 2016, the Florida Statewide Nuisance Alligator Program (SNAP) had to remove 8,050 alligators who had walked onto human property.

CHAINSAWS AND BULLDOZERS

Habitat loss happens in several ways. There may be a full-scale attack on nature, using chainsaws or fire to strip a forest, or bulldozers and concrete to build a huge dam. Or there may be a gradual degradation of the environment, due to pollution by industrial waste, the diversion of water resources, or over-grazing by livestock. Every bit as dangerous, but often less obvious, is fragmentation. As a city grows, suburbs are built. Natural habitats become islands, cut off from each other. Animal populations become isolated, with fewer breeding possibilities. Roads are built across migration routes, and the city still grows and grows.

CROWDED PLANET

In 1800, about 1 billion people lived in the world. At that time, an Industrial Revolution was underway in Europe and North America. This was a period marked by new factories, railway building, and the growth of big cities. It was also the beginning of a human assault on the environment, which is still spreading around the world today.

SOARING NUMBERS

The rise of industry was matched by a very steep rise in human population. By 1960, we numbered 3 billion, and today we have more than doubled that, at about 7.4 billion. And every five minutes, another 2,150 more babies are born. By the year 2050, the global population should be about 9.7 billion. By 2100, perhaps 11.2 billion. The population numbers are then expected to level off – but there are still many unknown factors.

A satellite image shows the urban sprawl of Shanghai in China. The city is one of the most populous in the world with around 24 million inhabitants.

ICEBERG AHEAD – FOR NOW

A cruise liner in the Arctic Ocean sails past an iceberg. Global warming means that more icebergs are breaking away from Arctic glaciers and are melting more quickly once in the sea.

HUMAN IMPACT

Is the world too crowded? Well, physically, there is still plenty of room on the planet. It is more a question of where people live and how people live and use the land. Cities are growing bigger and bigger as people pour into them from the countryside. This is called urbanization. More people use more precious resources. Industry is still polluting the planet and fossil fuels such as oil, gas, and coal contribute to global warming (see pages 16–17).

ACTION PLANS

Today, humans understand far more about the environment and population than ever before. Conservation and the environment are discussed by the world"s politicians. But are they doing too little, too late?

LET'S DISCUSS...
POPULATION GROWTH

- could be reduced if we tackle poverty.
- could be handled with better land use.
- will stabilize over the next 100 years.

- increases urbanization.
- increases pressure on resources and habitats.
- will still be very large over the next 100 years.

11

HUNGER AND THIRST

As the population grows, supplies of food and water will have to be stretched further. In the next decade, 1.8 billion people might find themselves short of water according to the UN (United Nations). Also, farmers may need to grow 70 percent more crops to feed so many people.

This is an aerial view of a huge oil palm plantation. The intensive cultivation of palm oil results in deforestation and the destruction of biodiversity.

DRINKING THE LANDSCAPE DRY

Humans will need more water for drinking, irrigating crops, watering their herds, industry, and sanitation. There are new aquifers or water sources available, but these may be too expensive to drill and maintain, too difficult to reach, or not have enough water for a long-term supply. As water is pumped out, the level of underground water drops. Plants die off, and the water holes where wild animals come to drink run dry. If plant roots no longer trap moisture, the soil may turn to dust or desert.

DISAPPEARING WATER
Giraffes bend their necks to drink at a water hole in Kenya. As water supplies dry up, animals have to travel farther in order to survive.

"We abuse land because we regard it as a commodity belonging to us. When we see land as a community to which we belong, we may begin to use it with love and respect."

Aldo Leopold, US conservationist (1887–1948)

MORE FARMING, FEWER FORESTS

The need for food may encourage overfishing of the world's oceans. Extra crops need land, which may mean that more forests are cut down or burnt, or more grasslands ploughed up. Intensive farming may be encouraged, using more chemicals on the land. New strains of hardier crops may be specially produced by genetic modification (GM), although critics fear these might affect nearby wild plants and animals, reducing biodiversity.

RICE PADDIES
Flooded rice fields, called paddies, arranged in terraces on the island of Bali, Indonesia. Compared to crops such as rice or wheat, beef production per calorie needs 160 times more land and creates 11 times more greenhouse gases.

CLEVER SOLUTIONS?

There are other ways of looking at this problem. Cutting down the vast mountains of food that currently go to waste would be a big help, or reducing the amount of water that people in developed countries splash around their bathrooms. Or what about changing land use? Turning over cattle ranching to crops with a high nutritional value would save money, save water, feed the world — and save rich habitats for biodiversity.

LET'S DISCUSS...
NEW FARMING

• could be reduced by cutting food waste.

• could focus more on food crops and less on cattle.

• could be more environment-friendly.

• could destroy more natural habitats.

• could become more intensive and industrialized.

• could divert more water for irrigation.

13

1 DRIVEN TO DESTRUCTION

Powerful economic forces drive habitat destruction, as well as human need. The world's natural resources are made into all the goods we buy and sell and use, from cars to smartphones and jewelry. There's money in the ground – until these resources run out.

Acid rain has destroyed trees on the border between the Czech Republic and the mountains of Poland. The burning of fossil fuel and its toxic emissions can lead to acid rain.

A WORLDWIDE PROBLEM

People often kill wild animals for their fur or their hide, or just for fun with guns. Few of the world's biomes are safe from humans. Oil and gas are extracted in the deserts of Southwest Asia, in the rainforests of the Niger Delta in West Africa, in the South China Sea, and even in the frozen Arctic. Metal ores are mined in every continent, often leaving behind toxic waste and a ravaged landscape. The loggers don't just destroy the tropical forests, but also the swampy forests in the far north of Russia and the Tasmanian forests in Australia.

WEARING FURS

Some people think that wearing animal fur, such as the fur of a beaver, is fashionable and shows how wealthy they are, while others believe it is wrong to kill an animal just for its fur.

WHAT ABOUT THE ECONOMY?

The products and by-products of these human activities are simply the things we use everyday. Manufacturing creates employment and wealth. Our factories produce life-saving medicines and TVs. Economic development can relieve poverty and reduce population growth.

OPEN MINING

Mining for precious stones called opals can be difficult and dangerous work. The landscape around Coober Pedy, Australia (above), is filled with shafts and pits.

LESS IS MORE

Is there a conflict of interests here, of people versus planet? A different understanding of our planet could provide a solution. Careful forest management can provide a sustainable source of timber. New technologies can reduce water consumption or fossil fuel emissions. Do we need to produce more and more "stuff"?

LET'S DISCUSS...
MINING, DRILLING AND LOGGING

- provide work for many people.
- give us many useful products.
- drive economic growth.

- use up finite resources.
- can permanently destroy natural habitats.
- may pollute the environment on a massive scale.

"A society is defined not only by what it creates, but by what it refuses to destroy."

John C Sawhill, US economist and conservationist (1936 - 2000)

15

THE WARMING PLANET

A digger that tears up roots and gouges out soil is an obvious destroyer of the habitat. Global warming is rather less obvious, but i is the greatest environmental problem facing the world this century. Climate defines our biomes, ecosystems, and habitats. If that changes, then living species have to either move or adapt—or become extinct.

GLOBAL GREENHOUSE

Greenhouse gases in the atmosphere trap energy from the Sun, helping to warm the planet.
1. Radiation travels through space from the Sun and is absorbed by Earth.
2. Some of the Sun's energy is reflected back out into space.
3. Some gases in the atmosphere trap the energy and reflect it back, where it warms the planet up even further.

THE BIG HEAT

Since 1900, the Earth's average temperature has risen by 1.53°F (0.85°C). Recent years have seen records broken, and the temperatures are expected to keep rising. Most scientists agree that this is happening because emissions of gases such as carbon dioxide (CO_2) and methane (CH_4) are becoming trapped in the Earth's atmosphere. The gases are blocking solar radiation that is being reflected from the Earth. Because of their warming effect, these are known as greenhouse gases.

HABITATS IN DANGER

CO_2 is released by burning fossil fuels such as oil, gas, and coal. Normally this gas is absorbed by forests, oceans, and soil, but the increase in emissions from transportation, power stations, and factories has overloaded the system. Habitat destruction, such as the clearance of forests, only makes the situation worse. Habitats may be affected by drought, heatwaves, flooding, melting ice, severe tropical storms, unpredictable weather, and rising sea levels. The oceans are becoming more acidic. Food supply, breeding sites, and migration patterns may be upset. The extent of environmental damage will depend on the future rise in temperature.

NUMBER CRUNCH
In 2015, the climate conference in Paris set a target of limiting climate temperature increase to well below 3.6°F (2°C). By 2017, that figure was already very hard to meet. An increase of over 5.4°F (3°C) will make many animals go extinct.

A huge traffic jam in the city of Hyderabad in India. Exhaust fumes from cars and trucks add to the buildup of greenhouse gases.

LET'S DISCUSS... CLIMATE CHANGE

- will disturb and destroy habitats.
- is already under way and cannot be stopped immediately.
- could affect the world for centuries to come.

- could make many animals go extinct.
- is making the oceans more acidic.
- is made worse by deforestation.

17

ANIMALS OVER PEOPLE?

The East African savannah is the habitat of some of the world's last great herds of wildebeest, elephants, giraffes, and zebras, and also of fierce predators such as crocodiles and lions. They mostly live within national parks where they are protected. But the parks are also a meeting point with the often hostile world of humans. Whose interests should come first? Those of the animals, the local people, or the tourists?

WILDLIFE SURVIVAL is a priority for the planet and its biodiversity. The parks should be for the exclusive use of wild animals.

SHOULD LEGALIZED HUNTING by rich foreigners be allowed in wildlife refuges?

IN RECENT YEARS, there have been plans to build a new highway to the Serengeti plains of Tanzania and a new railway through Kenya's Nairobi National Park. The park is already being fragmented and fenced because it is so close to the city. Such projects could be barriers to the great seasonal migration routes.

THE ANIMALS LIVING in the national parks of Kenya and Tanzania are among the most wonderful sights on the planet. It is absolutely essential that they are protected from poachers who kill elephants for their ivory and rhinoceroses for their horns.

QUESTION IT!
SHOULD THE INTERESTS OF WILD ANIMALS COME BEFORE THOSE OF PEOPLE?

> "The Masai always come in third, behind tourism and conservation."
>
> Damian Bell, Honeyguide Foundation of Tanzania

Tourists in off-road vehicles photograph elephants, lions and cheetahs in Kenya's Masai Mara game reserve.

TOURISM PROVIDES the funds needed for conservation. It can be educational, enabling people to learn about the importance of biodiversity and conservation. Much better cameras than guns! The more money local people can make from tourism, the less likely they are to turn to poaching.

OVER THE YEARS, communities of the Masai, who live in Kenya and Tanzania, have been forced to relocate their homes and cattle outside national park borders. This has caused them much suffering. The Masai are experts at coexisting with wild animals and can play an important part in protecting the habitat.

A NATURAL SAVANNAH landscape has always included humans. They are a natural part of the ecosystem.

A NEW HIGHWAY MIGHT benefit the local economy, and can be planned to minimize disruption of wildlife.

DOES MASS TOURISM, with its hotels, camps, lodges, safari vans, and cameras, interfere with the natural habitat?

19

OCEANS AND COASTS

Earth is known as the blue planet. 71 percent of the planet's surface is covered in oceans, brimming with salty water. Ocean currents between the North and South poles and the Equator help to control climate, and water from the oceans falls as rain. The marine habitat supports a vast number of species, many of them still unclassified.

A humpback whale in Kenai Fjords National Park, Alaska. The species' numbers had fallen to around 5,000 prior to the commercial hunting ban of 1966, and numbers have since increased to around 80,000.

ALL IS NOT WELL

In 2015, 737 marine creatures were on the IUCN Red List (see pages 28-29) as being threatened or endangered. There are probably many more. Marine protected areas are vital for conserving marine habitats, but they only cover about 4 percent of the world's oceans.

NUMBER CRUNCH

In 2010, the *Deepwater Horizon* oil platform exploded in the Gulf of Mexico. It spilled over 150 million gallons (570 million l) of oil and polluted up to 67,950 square miles (176,000 km²). About 12 percent of brown pelicans and 32 percent of laughing gulls may have been killed. Dolphin deaths off Louisiana quadrupled in the years that followed.

SEAS OR SEWERS?

Earth's oceans face many threats. Huge "factory" trawlers reduce fish stocks at a rate that is unsustainable. Tankers spill black sticky oil into the ocean. Sewage and toxic chemicals pollute the sea. Tiny specks of plastics used in industry collect in the oceans and are swallowed by fish. Tropical coasts are stripped of their mangrove forests, which offer a rich habitat and form a natural defence against flooding. Tourist resorts and coastal cities cover shores in concrete.

OIL DAMAGE

A team of environmentalists cleans up an oil spill on Huntington Beach, California. Oil spills have devastating consequences for marine life.

TEMPERATURES RISING

The oceans absorb CO_2 naturally, but excessive levels are causing acidification, which damages coral reefs and seashells. The oceans are about 1.8 °F (1°C) warmer than they were 140 years ago, which affects the marine organisms on which fish and whales feed. Warm water expands, raising sea levels. This is made worse by the melting of ice in the Arctic and Antarctic. Sea flooding erodes coasts and can further damage beaches where turtles and some sea birds lay their eggs.

LET'S DISCUSS... CORAL REEFS

- are the most diverse marine ecosystems.
- benefit about 25 percent of ocean species.
- are among the most beautiful sights on the planet.

- are threatened by climate change.
- are threatened by pollution.
- are threatened by tourism.

2 WETLANDS AND DRY LANDS

The first human civilizations grew up beside great rivers and lakes, where there was water for drinking and watering crops. These were rich natural habitats, but over the ages many became contaminated with sewage. Many were turned into canals and polluted with chemicals and garbage. Huge concrete dams were built, which blocked the route for migratory fish, such as salmon.

Lake Drummond is at the center of the Great Dismal Swamp, a marshy region of North Carolina and Virginia.

NUMBER CRUNCH

The waters of the Aral Sea in Central Asia, once the world's fourth largest lake, were diverted for irrigation.

• In 1960, the Aral Sea had an area of 26,250 square miles (68,000 km²).

• By 2004, it had dwindled to a number of small lakes with a total area of 6,625 square miles (17,160 km²).

• Measures to reduce water loss include the building of a huge dam and by 2016, after almost disappeariing, water was returned to one of two small remaining lakes.

Aral Sea

Coastline area 1960

Coastline area 2010

VANISHING WETLANDS

Wetland habitats include river basins and deltas, peat bogs, marshes, swamps, flood plains, lakes, mud flats, and salt marshes. They are filled with an amazing variety of plants, birds, insects, fish, mammals, and reptiles. Wetlands form a useful buffer zone in areas that flood — and more flooding may be on the way as a result of climate change. They also serve as aquifers, providing water for humans and livestock. Today, wetlands have been drained for building or farming, polluted or sprayed to clear them of dangerous insects such as the mosquitoes that pass on malaria. The numbers of animals living in these habitats may have dropped by as much as 76 percent since 1970.

INVASION
Water hyacinth is an invasive aquatic plant that can cover lakes and wetland habitats. It can affect water flow, block sunlight, and starve the water of oxygen, killing fish in the process.

DESERT HOTSPOTS

Global warming could make wet places wetter and dry places drier. Deserts and other dry regions are expected to spread with global warming. They already cover one quarter of the Earth's surface. Mining in deserts can further destabilize fragile soils. Hotter desert soils could lose nitrogen, which helps existing desert plants survive. Desert animals and plants have become finely tuned to the slightest changes in temperature and water supplies — and might yet teach humans useful lessons about adapting to hot, dry conditions.

DESERT LIFE
Gemsbok, a type of large antelope, are well adapted to the harsh life in the Namibian desert. They have broad hooves to walk across the sand and white bellies to reflect heat from the ground.

LET'S DISCUSS...
WETLANDS

- are a natural means of flood control.
- are natural filters and purifiers of water.
- stabilize shore lines by acting as a barrier between the sea and the land.

- have been drained for farming and building.
- have had water diverted for irrigation of crops.
- have been polluted by chemicals used in farming.

TUNDRA, GRASSLANDS, AND FORESTS

The tundra region around the Arctic Circle is bitterly cold, with very few trees. Normally only the surface of the ground melts in the brief summer, while the deeper soil stays frozen all year round. Global warming has caused this permafrost to melt and release methane, a greenhouse gas, into the atmosphere. The fragile tundra habitat is threatened with industrial development, oil drilling, and pollution.

SEAS OF GRASS?

Natural grasslands once occupied 25 percent of land on Earth, but from the 1700s into modern times, they were mostly taken over for agriculture or ranching. They include the prairies of North America, the steppes of Eastern Europe and Central Asia, and the South American pampas. Environmental risk comes from invasive species, fragmentation, over-intensive farming and soil erosion — the US prairies turned into a dustbowl in the 1930s. Temperatures on the steppes of Mongolia have risen by 3.42°F (1.9°C) over the past 60 years.

NUMBER CRUNCH

At least 30 million bison grazed the North American prairies when Europeans first arrived. By 1885, only 600 or so survived. With the reduction of hunting, numbers increased, and today there are about 30,000 in the wild and 400,000 on farms.

Large grasslands are perfect for growing crops and are home to super-sized farms, such as this one in Canada.

SAVANNAH DROUGHT

The climate risk to the tree-dotted savannah grasslands of East and Southern Africa is longer and more severe drought, leading in places to desertification. As cattle herders leave the land for the cities, urban development spreads, fragmenting the environment and using up dwindling supplies of water.

FEEL THE HEAT
The savannah of Kruger National Park in South Africa is a dry and harsh environment. Summer days are hot and temperatures often soar above 100°F (38°C).

BUSHFIRE
Dry conditions can lead to the rapid spread of fire, which can totally destroy the landscape.

FORESTS AND FIRES

Climate change can increase the risk of devastating wildfire. Over 30 percent of land is taken up by forest. Only six percent of that is rainforest, yet that is where 40–75 percent of all living species are found.

These are great green oxygen machines, which soak up the CO_2.

Forests are cut down not only for timber, often illegally, but for growing crops, ranching, and settlement. New roads give hunters access to new areas where they can kill wild animals, such as monk-eys, for food or "bush meat." Mining, often illegal and dangerous, can poison forest rivers.

LET'S DISCUSS...
NATURAL GRASSLANDS

- can have 100 or more plant species in five acres.
- can support large herds of grazing animals.
- can support burrowing rodents such as prairie dogs.

- are only protected in five percent of the total area worldwide.
- are areas of low rainfall, so at risk of drought.
- are easily over-grazed or over-farmed.

2 INTRODUCING SPECIES

In 1788, British settlers arrived in Australia with some caged rabbits for food. In 1859, a few were released so they could be hunted for sport. By the 1920s, there were 10 billion of them. The Australians built a 2,021-mile-long (3,253 km) fence to stop them from spreading. It didn't work. They shot rabbits by the million, but that didn't work either. They poisoned them with a deadly virus called myxoma. That worked for a bit, but 40 years later their numbers were back up to 300 million.

WHO DOESN'T LIKE CUTE LITTLE BUNNIES? Australian farmers, because rabbits munch on their crops and pastures. Rabbits have devastated Australia's unique environment, nibbling away at tree bark, shrubs, and seedlings. Rabbits took over the burrows of native species and competed with them for food, which was bad news for species of wombats and rock kangaroos.

MANY INVASIVE SPECIES ARRIVE BY ACCIDENT. Rats escaping from old sailing ships devastated wildlife on many islands. Tourists returning home may bring in foreign insects. Animals from pet stores and zoos may escape and breed.

THEN THE CANE TOADS were introduced into Australia in 1935 in order to kill the beetles that attack the sugar cane crop. Today, they number about 200 million. They poison many reptiles that eat them, compete with native species, and spread animal diseases.

QUESTION IT!

IS IT WRONG TO INTRODUCE NEW SPECIES INTO A HABITAT?

NOT ALL INTRODUCED SPECIES

spell doom and gloom. Many have no harmful effects on the environment. For example, in Britain, the rainbow trout, common pheasant, Canada goose, and midwife toad have all been introduced without problems.

NUMBER CRUNCH

Cats everywhere attack wild birds and rodents in extraordinary numbers. In the US, pet and feral cats are believed to kill between 1.3 and 4 billion wild birds per year.

MOST OF THE CROPS

we grow originally came from other parts of the world, but were introduced to provide food or drink. Do we worry too much about whether a natural species is native to the area or not? Is it ethical to kill animals that are doing no harm to the habitat, simply on the grounds they are a non-native species?

BRINGING IN ANIMALS

to destroy pests was a method of habitat control being used in Egypt 3,000 years ago, when cats were used to destroy rodents in grain stores. If importation causes no problems, at least the use of toxic pesticides or weedkillers can be avoided. But it's vital that complex ecosystems are fully understood, because if mistakes are made, a disastrous new situation may arise.

The cane toad was introduced into Australia from Hawaii. Its poisonous glands and toxic skin have killed many animals, and it is particularly dangerous to dogs.

ON THE RED LIST

Habitat destruction has many victims. They include some of the best known animals on the planet — the chimpanzee, the mountain gorilla, the blue whale, the snow leopard, the Indian elephant, and the Bengal tiger. Perhaps the most famous example is the giant panda, threatened by fragmentation of its habitat in the bamboo forests of southwest China.

IBERIAN LYNX

The Red List may include good news as well as bad, such as the recovery from the brink of extinction of the Iberian lynx, a big cat found in Spain and Portugal.

KAKAPO

The flightless parrot, the kakapo, was almost wiped out as a result of hunting, habitat clearance, and the introduction of predators, like the cat, into New Zealand. Conservationists now closely monitor the few remaining birds on three predator-free islands.

ASSESSING STATUS

The IUCN (International Union for Conservation of Nature) assesses the risk to species based on scientific data, and publishes a regular status report called the Red List.

Status is defined like this:

(1) Data Deficient
(that is, not enough known).
(2) Least Concern.
(3) Near Threatened.
(4) Threatened – Vulnerable, Endangered, or Critically Endangered.
(5) Extinct in the Wild.
(6) Extinct.

NUMBER CRUNCH

The 2016 IUCN Red List included assessments of 85,604 species of which 24,307 are threatened with extinction.

Threat of extinction

LIFE SUPPORT

Conservation success requires a lot of human intervention in the natural world. Management might include repairing damaged habitat, moving populations of animals, additional feeding, controlling predators, incubating bird eggs, and protecting sites. But in the end, improvement to habitat must be sustainable without a life-support system.

A mountain gorilla in the forests of Uganda in Africa. The eastern gorilla is a critically endangered species as a result of illegal hunting and the destruction of its habitat.

LET'S DISCUSS...
RISK FROM HABITAT LOSS

• can be reduced by research and repair.

• can be reduced by laws and protection.

• can be reduced by breeding programs.

• is made worse by collectors.

• is made worse by hunters.

• is made worse by the trade in endangered species.

3 DIVERSITY OR DEATH

When a habitat becomes fragmented or degraded, it can no longer support healthy breeding populations. Each species population needs to breed with other populations of the same species in order to bring about genetic variation. There also needs to be a broad variety of different species and enough living networks to create a rich and sustainable ecosystem. All these factors make up biodiversity.

THE BIO-CRASH

A crash in biodiversity leads to the extinction of a species, a full stop in its evolution as a life form — although other related species might carry forward part of its genetic history. We don't actually know how many species of animals and plants currently exist, although we are learning more all the time. Between 1.4 and 1.8 million are scientifically recognized at the moment. Even so, most scientists today think that the extinction rate is speeding up, and that the spread of human activities is the cause.

NUMBERCRUNCH

It is estimated that the extinction rate is already 1,000 times the natural or "background" rate, and may even rise to 10,000 times that rate.

IS THIS A DINOSAUR MOMENT?

It has been 66 million years since dinosaurs walked the Earth. We know from studying fossils that there have been at least five great mass extinctions during the 4.5-billion-year history of our planet, as well as many smaller ones. They may have been caused in the past by changes in climate and sea level, by volcanic activity and by changes in the chemicals of the atmosphere, or by impact with asteroids. Are we heading for a sixth human-made mass extinction?

LET'S DISCUSS... EXTINCTIONS

- are more easily predicted thanks to modern technology.
- can be prevented by intervention and conservation.
- can be prevented by improving biodiversity.

- are nevertheless increasing all the time.
- are at risk of increasing due to climate change.
- are mostly linked to habitat destruction.

The black-and-white ruffed lemur lives on the island of Madagascar. The destruction of the rainforest and hunting has threatened its survival as a species.

31

THE DODO

The small islands of the southern Indian Ocean are vulnerable to extinctions. Unique species evolved there in isolation, but had nowhere to go when things got tough. The dodo was last seen on Mauritius in 1662. It was a flightless relative of the pigeon and about the size of a turkey. It ate the fruit of the tambalacoque or dodo tree. Its habitat was disturbed, and it was hunted for food by passing sailors. Its nests and eggs were destroyed by introduced species such as cats, rats, dogs, and pigs.

THE DODO IS NOW FAMOUS for not being here anymore. It's a sad story. But does its extinction really matter, and if so, why?

BIODIVERSITY IS SO EASILY WHITTLED AWAY as habitats fragment or disappear. About 350 years after we said goodbye to the dodo, we are looking not just at one small island in trouble, but at environmental breakdown on a global scale.

HUMANS HAVE MUCH TO LOSE WHEN SPECIES BECOME EXTINCT. Plants may be useful as sources of new medicines and cures. Insects may be useful for pest control or pollination.

The dodo was discovered by Europeans on the island of Mauritius in 1598. Seen as a curiosity, some dodos were brought to Europe by wealthy collectors.

QUESTION IT!
DEAD AS A DODO!
BUT DOES IT
MATTER?

WE MAY TALK about living within the laws of nature, but don't scientists say that all living creatures have to adapt or die out?

THE BIGGEST MASS EXTINCTION of them all took place about 252 million years ago, when 96 percent of all marine species died out, as well as 70 percent of land species with backbones. It took them about 10 million years to recover.

NUMBER CRUNCH

There were once about 9 billion passenger pigeons in the US. The entire population was shot for meat or hunting between the 1850s and 1900. The last one of all died in Cincinnati Zoo in 1914.

OF ALL THE SPECIES EVER to have lived on Earth, about 99.9 percent are extinct today. Humans too will be just another fossil one day.

CONSERVATION IN ACTION

Many of the earliest religious beliefs and philosophies were rooted in respect for nature. Later, people learned to tame nature in gardens or parks, but came to see the wilderness as something dangerous, which needed to be conquered and plundered for resources. Scientific conservation first appeared in the 1800s, at the same time as habitat destruction became severe.

An anti-rhino-poaching unit in South Africa dart and capture a rhino in order to move it to a safer location. Rhinos are often hunted for their horns.

ORGANIZE!

The survival of Earth's natural environment depends on humans saving, protecting, or reclaiming wild habitats. Practical action can be taken by all of us as individuals, but also by local conservation societies, by the big environmental action groups such as Greenpeace and Friends of the Earth, by government and UN agencies. They can set up reserves and wildlife sanctuaries, or create habitat corridors to prevent fragmentation. We need to work locally and campaign globally.

THE BIGGER PICTURE

It is up to councils and governments to get a grip on urbanization and town planning. In the countryside, authorities should consider better ways of farming sustainably, using the land and producing food with less waste. In the least developed regions of the world, population and poverty are key issues when it comes to protecting the environment. Schools everywhere can play a part in teaching young people about protecting the environment, and encouraging them to take part in community projects such as tree planting or pond digging.

TREE PLANTING

Arbor Day is a day when people are encouraged to plant and care for trees. These children are planting trees in Oyster Bay, New York.

GREEN ARCTIC

The Greenpeace ship *Arctic Sunrise* documents climate change by surveying glaciers and recording sea temperatures. It has been involved in numerous environmental campaigns, including protests against whaling and the drilling of oil in the Arctic.

LET'S DISCUSS...
WHAT CAN WE DO?

- plant new forest.
- dig new ponds.
- plant flowers that attract insects.

- oppose bad planning in cities.
- boycott wood from unsustainable forests.
- campaign against food waste.

POWER AND PROGRESS

Individual farmers may have little control over the future of the environment. A small number of very powerful corporations are the big players. In 2016, the German company Bayer took over the US company Monsanto, known for its promotion of GM (genetically modified) crops. The new company will control 25 percent of all the world's crop seeds and pesticides. Its activities will affect natural habitats and farmlands.

GM CROP

A Monsanto GM farm crop. Many people accused the industrial giant Monsanto of marketing highly toxic products that contaminate the environment and cause poor health.

Danish citizens gather in Copenhagen as part of the Global Climate March, held on the eve of the United Nations climate summit in 2015. Hundreds of thousands of people around the world took to the streets.

INTERNATIONAL CONSERVATION

Habitat destruction is closely related to so many other global crises, from population growth and poverty to climate change, that policies of the United Nations are very important. The UN and many of its agencies, including the United Nations Environment Programme (UNEP), lead the way with a wide range of environmental action, including emission targets to reduce climate change, controlling pollution, managing ecosystems, regulation, and education. Many other international treaty organizations play an important part, particularly the European Union (EU), which has the widest range of laws protecting the environment and supporting sustainability.

"A point has been reached in history when we must shape our actions throughout the world with a more prudent care for their environmental consequences."

The Declaration of the UN Conference on the Human Environment (1972)

LET'S DISCUSS...

THE UNITED NATIONS

• can direct habitat protection through many agencies.

• can call world conferences on climate change.

• can uphold international law.

• can only do as much as its members allow it to.

• has interests that sometimes conflict with each other.

• is sometimes criticized as having too much power.

ZOOS AND CONSERVATION

The story of the great flood is well known by Jews, Christians, and Muslims. Similar stories first appeared in ancient Mesopotamia (modern Iraq). In all these versions, there is a great flood, and all the species of animals in the world are saved by putting them in a big boat called an ark. Is it acceptable to see zoos as modern versions of the ark? Can they save animal species from habitat destruction?

ZOOS MAY TAKE PART IN international programs for breeding species such as the giant panda. Some zoos may have plans for reintroducing captive animals into the wild.

THE NEAREST MOST OF US GET to a tiger or an ostrich is in a zoo. It's an amazing experience to see such an animal in real life. This is important for children, and many zoos offer an educational program for school visits. This may inspire children to become the conservationists of tomorrow.

QUESTION IT!
DO ZOOS HELP CONSERVE ENDANGERED ANIMAL SPECIES?

ZOOS OFFER THE CHANCE to study the anatomy and genetic makeup of endangered species, their behavior and feeding habits, and the way they reproduce.

THE FIRST ZOOS STARTED AS FREAK SHOWS, with little respect shown to the animals while the public came to gawp. It is still cruel and immoral to imprison animals.

CAPTIVE BREEDING IS OFTEN from a very limited gene pool, and animals bred in captivity often fare poorly when released into the wild. They may have little resistance to diseases they encounter in natural habitats. There have been few successful reintroductions to the wild.

ANIMAL BEHAVIOR IN CAPTIVITY is very different to how animals behave in the wild, so is of little use for serious study. Many animals become stressed or unhappy when caged.

Baby pandas take a nap. The survival of the giant panda species is totally reliant on conservation programs, many of them run by zoos.

MOST MODERN ZOOS have a much better idea of how to keep animals healthy and happy than in the old days, with more spacious enclosures and cages. Captive animals often live longer than in the wild. However, not all zoos are good and not all animals are suited for zoo life.

ZOO BREEDING OFTEN BEGINS TOO LATE, once the damage to habitat has already happened. The cost of keeping animals in zoos would be better spent on habitat conservation.

39

THE WORLD'S WILD PLACES

Humans evolved in natural environments, on the savannah, in forests, on the seashores and among the mountains. We still get a special and sometimes familiar feeling when we hike into the world's wild places. These are shrinking fast, though. About 1.2 million square miles (3.2 million km²) of wilderness has been lost in the last 20 years.

AN ANCIENT INSPIRATION

Even so, designated wilderness areas, often known as national parks or wildlife refuges, now protect natural habitats from destruction around the world. The world's oldest protected area is probably Bogd Khan Uul in Mongolia. It was protected as a holy mountain from about 800 years ago, and declared a national park in 1783. In 1996, it became a UNESCO Biosphere Reserve.

A breathtaking view of Yosemite National Park in California. The park's wilderness supports a diversity of plants and animals.

WOLVES RETURN

Wolves chase an elk in Yellowstone National Park in Wyoming. By the 1920s, the gray wolf had disappeared from the park, but was successfully reintroduced in the 1990s.

SAVE THE WILDERNESS

The modern movement to save the wilderness really took off in the United States, inspired by nature-lovers such as Henry David Thoreau (1817-62) and John Muir (1838-1914). The first US National Park was Yellowstone, Wyoming, founded in 1872. Today, it is home to over 60 species of mammal and 300 species of bird, in addition to reptiles, amphibians, fish, and insects. The largest US National Park and Preserve is Wrangell-St. Elias in Alaska, at 20,587 square miles (53,321 km²).

FUTURE BIODIVERSITY

A protected wilderness is probably the most valuable resource the planet has to offer. The wild lands may hold the real prize, a key to future biodiversity. Parks are of course just oases in a damaged world, but there is always hope.

"What would the world be, once bereft
Of wet and of wildness? Let them be left,
O let them be left, wildness and wet:
Long live the weeds and the wilderness yet."

From "Inversnaid" (1881) by English poet
Gerard Manley Hopkins

LET'S DISCUSS... REFUGES AND NATIONAL PARKS

- can protect ancient habitats.
- can restore damaged habitats and reintroduce key species.
- can introduce city dwellers to the natural world.

- now cover 10–15 percent of the Earth's land surface.
- number over 161,000 sites.
- are on the increase around the world.

SEEDS OF THE FUTURE

The Royal Botanic Gardens in London has over 30,000 different kinds of living plants. In their refrigerated vaults at the Millennium Seed Bank Partnership in Sussex, UK, they have a global collection of nearly 2 billion seeds, covering over 13 percent of all the wild plant species in the world.

HOT HOUSE

This is the tropical Waterlily House in London's Kew Gardens. These botanical gardens house the most diverse collection of plants and fungi in the world and are now a UNESCO World Heritage site.

BANKS OF BIODIVERSITY

Another seed bank with a capacity for 2.5 billion seeds is buried in the icy permafrost of Spitsbergen, an island in the Norwegian Arctic. This one stores all the precious strains of food crops. There are banks of biodiversity around the world, as an insurance against any future environmental catastrophe.

NEW SOLUTIONS?

The creation of wilderness reserves and seed banks are great examples of just how clever humans can be. The planet will need these skills more than ever during the coming century. Important advances in the way we generate and store electricity are already happening, and these will help in the way we deal with climate change. But there is no magic wand to make everything right immediately. Much of the scientific effort will go into dealing with damage already done, and that is certainly true of endangered habitats. When it comes to the environment, it can take a lot of time and effort to change people's minds.

SUN POWER

Advances in solar energy technology mean even parts of the world that don't receive much sunlight can now use solar power, such as this farm in the United Kingdom.

The Svalbard Global Seed Vault is a secure seed bank on the Norwegian island of Spitsbergen. It provides a safety net in the event of a regional or global catastrophe.

"The more clearly we can focus our attention on the wonders and realities of the universe about us, the less taste we shall have for destruction."

Rachel Carson,
US conservationist
(1907–1964)

LET'S DISCUSS...
IN THE FUTURE

- we will have a greater understanding of biodiversity.
- we will be developing new, clean and sustainable technologies.
- we can extend and enforce habitat protection.

- there will be great environmental changes.
- there may be more conflict linked to the environment.
- there are many unknowns and factors that are hard to predict.

43

ECONOMY OR ECO-FRIENDLY?

Do environmentalists live in the real world? Economic growth cannot be achieved without making full use of all the resources the world has to offer. Or is it the miners and loggers who don't live in the real world? If we cannot stop the reckless use of finite resources, their "economic growth" cannot be maintained.

IF GETTING RID OF POVERTY is the best way to reduce population growth, we need economic growth. Everywhere. Making money means drilling for oil in the Arctic, fracking, clearing more farmland, dredging rivers, building new cities. It's what we're good at.

DO WE REALLY WANT to be the first generation in human history to leave the world a less developed place for our children?

HUMANS SHOULD STOP hanging their heads in shame and be proud of historic achievements such as cars and skyscrapers.

YOU CAN'T MAKE AN OMELETTE WITHOUT BREAKING EGGS. The Earth has put up with human interference for an awfully long time, and its ecosystems and habitats can take the pressure for many years to come.

QUESTION IT!
IS THERE REALLY A CONFLICT BETWEEN "PROGRESS" AND THE ENVIRONMENT?

NOBODY INTENDS TO GO BACKWARDS. The houses of the future will be high-tech, with the materials from which they are made generating their own power. That is already possible, and is a technical achievement we should all be proud of. Electric cars are already coming up fast on the outside lane.

UNLESS WE SORT OUT HOW to live on this planet, we will be staring our own extinction in the face.

HABITAT DESTRUCTION makes things worse not just for plants and wildlife, but for all of us.

Victoria Falls, or Mosi-oa-Tunya, on the border of Zambia and Zimbabwe in southern Africa. It is one of the Seven Natural Wonders of the World.

SUSTAINABILITY IS THE KEY TO GROWTH. Economic growth that creates unnecessary goods, wastes resources, and destroys the natural world offers no future worth passing on to future generations.

45

GLOSSARY

ACID RAIN

Rain with water molecules that have mixed with suplhur dioxide (SO_2) and nitrogen oxide (NO) emitted from factories and other industrial sites. The water becomes acidic, damaging trees, plants, and even buildings.

AQUIFER

A layer of underground rock, gravel, or soil that absorbs and stores water. This water can be accessed by digging wells into the aquifer. It may be raised to the surface by natural pressure or by pumping.

BIODIVERSITY

The range and variety of living organisms that live in a particular area.

BIOME

A large-scale ecological community that covers a major area. Biomes are usually defined by the types of plant that dominate them. They include grasslands, as well as deciduous forests and coniferous forests.

CARBON DIOXIDE (CO_2)

An odorless and colorless gas that is found in the atmosphere. It is released by all living things during a process called respiration, but absorbed by plants during a process called photosynthesis, which also uses water and sunlight to produce sugar and oxygen (O_2).

CONSERVATION

Protecting and saving the environment. This can take the form of repairing damaged ecosystems or preventing them from getting damaged.

ENVIRONMENTALIST

A person who tries to protect the environment. Actions might include preventing damage to habitats and ecosystems, or cleaning up the effects of pollution.

EQUATOR

The imaginary line that runs around Earth at its widest part.

EXTINCTION

When a species of living thing dies out and disappears forever, either in a specific region or from the entire planet.

FOSSIL FUEL

Fuel that is made from the ancient decayed remains of plants and animals. Fossil fuels include oil, coal, gas, and peat. They are burned to release energy in power stations and cars.

GENETICALLY MODIFIED

Describing a plant or animal that has had the genetic information in its DNA changed to give it different characteristics. This is usually done to improve how it grows or behaves. For example, it can make something more resistant to diseases or it can improve how much a crop produces.

GLOBAL WARMING

Any gradual increase in Earth's overall temperature. Most scientists believe current global warming is due to an increase in the levels of carbon dioxide in the atmosphere, which have been released by human activities, such as burning fossil fuels.

GREENHOUSE GAS

Any of the gases, such as carbon dioxide (CO_2) and methane (CH_4), which trap reflected radiation from the Sun in Earth's atmosphere, causing global warming.

FRAGMENTATION

When a plant or an animal's natural habitat becomes altered or isolated, for example by creeping urbanization or the conversion of land for farming, causing species numbers to decline, or to become extinct.

HABITAT

The type of natural environment in which a living thing lives and grows.

INDUSTRIAL REVOLUTION

The period of social and economic change brought on by the introduction of powered tools and machinery. It started in the late 1700s in the US and saw the growth of major towns and cities across the world.

MALARIA

A disease that is carried by some mosquito parasites and passed onto people when they are bitten. The disease attacks blood cells and causes fever, vomiting, headaches, coma, and even death.

MASS EXTINCTION

A period when a great number of extinctions occur. The dinosaurs died out in a mass extinction event about 66 million years ago, and some people believe that we are now entering another mass extinction event caused by humans.

PALM OIL

A type of edible vegetable oil that comes from the oil palm and is used in a wide range of products from fuels and foods to cosmetics and soaps. Many people believe that the growth in palm oil use is causing large-scale environmental damage as huge areas of rainforest are cleared to make room for enormous plantations.

PERMAFROST

A layer of soil that is frozen all year round. Permafrost is found in tundra and polar regions and can stretch down for hundreds of metres below the surface.

POACHER

A person who hunts animals illegally. Poachers kill animals for their meat, their skins or fur, or for specific body parts that are used in traditional medicine or to make ornaments. For example, poachers kill elephants to take their tusks.

POLES

The areas at the top and bottom of the planet. The North Pole and South Pole form the axis around which Earth spins.

POLLINATION

When male and female plant cells fuse together and fertilize. The male cells, or pollen, are usually carried to other plants by insects, but they can also be carried by the wind and water.

RAINFOREST

A region of forest that receives a large amount of rain throughout the year. Tropical rainforests are found near the Equator, while temperate rainforests are usually found near coasts.

RED LIST

Created by the International Union for Conservation of Nature (IUCN), this is a list of species whose survival is under threat. It records the status of each species and the particular problems it faces.

SAVANNAH

An ecosystem of open grasslands with scattered trees, and a dry and a rainy season.

SPECIES

Any particular and unique life form whose members look and behave in the same way and can mate and breed with each other to produce fertile offspring.

TROPICAL

Used to describe the regions that lie on either side of the Equator.

TUNDRA

Cold regions where the soil beneath the surface is permafrost and remains frozen all year round. This stops trees and other large plants growing. Tundra is found in regions around the Arctic and on a few Antarctic islands, as well as in areas high on mountains.

UNITED NATIONS (UN)

An international treaty organization where countries coordinate to encourage peace and cooperation. It was formed in 1945 after the end of the Second World War and its headquarters are in New York City.

INDEX